Teacher's Guide

Lessons to Help Children
Grow More as Christians

Written by: Lorraine Dick
Project editor: Kathryn Balzer

Winnipeg, MB, Canada / Hillsboro, KS, U.S.A.

First Steps for Kids

Copyright 1995 by
Kindred Productions,
Winnipeg, MB Canada

Published simultaneously by Kindred Productions, Winnipeg, Manitoba R2L 2E5 and Kindred Productions, Hillsboro Kansas, 67063 and the Board of Christian Education Ministries, Winnipeg, Manitoba R2L 2E5.

All rights reserved. With the exception of brief excerpts for reviews, no part of this book may be reproduced without the written permission of the publisher.

Cover and Book Design by
Reg Dick, R.J. Dick Design,
Vancouver, British Columbia

Printed in Canada by
The Christian Press, Winnipeg
Bowne of Vancouver, Vancouver

International Standard Book Number: 0-921788-19-3

Scripture taken from the Holy Bible, New International Version, Copyright© 1973, 1978, 1984 International Bible Society. Used by permission of Zondervan Bible Publishers.

Contents

Introduction 4

Note to Teacher 5

How To Use this Book 7

Lessons

    Belonging to a New Family 8

    Getting to Know God 16

    Bible Reading and Prayer 24

    Belonging at Church 32

Resource List 40

Sample Letters 41

About the Author 43

Introduction

It is always a thrill when children make decisions to follow Jesus. But what happens next?

Taking steps with Jesus is a metaphor to help children understand that following Jesus is a life-long journey. Assurance of salvation and understanding who God is provide the foundation for further steps. Prayer and Bible reading are not just things that Christians do but rather means of relating to God who loves and cares for each one.

First Steps for Kids is designed to teach life-long practices that will inspire children to take continued steps with Jesus. The four lessons are aimed at children ages seven to eleven. This program will help affirm and meet the faith needs of young believers.

You will find that the lessons are interactive; inviting the children to share their ideas and experiences. As the teacher, you have the privilege of sharing your relationship with Christ in a way that the children can understand and emulate.

"Go and make disciples, teaching them to obey all that I have commanded you... I am with you always" Matthew 28

Kathryn Balzer
Project Editor

Note to Teacher

The following information will help you plan for an effective **First Steps** program.

Who should teach this program?

Any adult who has a vibrant relationship with Jesus and who has a love for children is the ideal teacher. We suggest an experienced Sunday School teacher or a children's ministry director/pastor.

When should this program be taught?

Any time is a good time. It's a good idea to teach this program sometime in fall after summer camp and VBS programs are over. This will give time to connect with those leaders to find out which children have made a decision for Christ. **First Steps** can be taught as a pull out program from Sunday School or weekly club meetings.

How should children be invited to participate?

- Make a general announcement by describing that the program is for children who have made a decision to follow Christ and want to take further steps with Jesus.

- Invite children between the ages of seven and eleven to participate.

- Indicate the starting date, location of the classroom and how the children should contact you if they are interested. Since their decision to follow Jesus is individual, it is best if children make their own decision to join.

- Make special invitations for those children whose names you have gathered from camp or VBS program leaders.

- Contact the children's parents to let them know about **First Steps.** See the sample letter on page 41.

- Provide information sheets with a tear off to drop into your mailbox with their responses. See the sample note on page 42.

What supplies will I need?

- Each child should have their own copy of the **First Steps for Kids: Student Guide**. The Guide will be needed in each of the lessons and also provides at-home activity options. The **Student Guide** is intended to give children the option of recording prayers and responses to Bible reading at home. Explore the pages of the **Student Guide** with the children and encourage them to use the various formats for prayer and Bible reading.
- You will find a list of what you need in each lesson.

How should the classroom be set up?

- Make your classroom an exciting space for the children. Use posters and bulletin boards to add color.
- If possible, set up the room so that you can do activities on the floor as well as at a table.
- A chalk board or chart paper will be necessary for most lessons.

Are there any other details that I should know?

Limit the class size to ten. This will give you and the students the opportunity to get to know each other personally.

Encourage the children by giving them a phone call during the week, or sending them a post card to remind them of your prayers. If possible, be in contact with the children in the weeks after the program. Your ongoing encouragement will be significant to their growth.

Be in contact with children's teachers and leaders so that they can be included in the recruitment and development of the program.

Remember, Christianity is about being in a relationship with God. The simplicity of the lessons is meant to allow you to develop a warm relationship with a small group of children, and thus show them that their Christian walk is indeed a relationship with their heavenly Father.

How to Use this Book

Each lesson is divided into five major sections. The following is a general outline of what you will find in each lesson. **Text that is in bold print is what you may say to the children.**

Teacher Preparation

Use this section for personal reflection. Read the scripture and ask God to guide you as you teach. The children will watch you carefully and will respond to the sincerity of your heart.

What You Need

You will find a list of all the things you need to implement the lesson. In many cases, the items will be listed again in the part of the lesson where they are required. Gather the items in advance so that you can be ready.

Goals
The overall intention is stated at the beginning of each lesson.

Opener *(time allotments are marked at the beginning of each major section)*

Each class begins with an activity that you will do with the children. Use this time to welcome the children and get to know them. There are activity options. Choose the one that suits you best. Each activity is intended to provide an introduction to the main idea of the lesson.

Objectives
Learning objectives are outlined for each lesson.

Teaching/Learning

This is the main learning section of the lesson. Sometimes there is more than one activity to work through. You will find the instructions laid out in a step by step, easy to follow format.

Some activities involve filling in responses in the **Student Guide**. Page numbers and instructions are given.

Often children will be invited to "brainstorm" or share their ideas with the class. Use open-ended questions to gather their ideas and give enough time to explore thoughts. This is a wonderful opportunity for you to hear and affirm what the children already know.

Teacher Tip
These will provide you with insights and ideas to improve your presentation of the lesson.

Conclusion

This is your opportunity to make summary statements. You could also ask a student to share what they have learned.

Each lesson has its own particular "at home" activity. Direct the children to these activities as well as the other Journal pages found in the **Student Guide**.

1 Belonging to a New Family

Teacher Preparation
Read: Romans 8:12-17

Belonging. Every person has the need to belong. While we did not choose to belong to our human family, we can choose to be part of God's family.

God invites us to belong to his family. Belonging in God's family enables members to have the assurance of forgiveness, new life and hope.

Reflect on your own coming into the family of God. Prepare to share the joy of belonging with the group of children in your class.

Prayer:
Lord, you know my deep need to belong. I need to belong to you so that I can show these children about the joy of knowing you. Amen.

What You Need
- **Student Guide** for each child
- pencils, markers/crayons
- extra Bibles
- mural paper to cover table or wall
- jelly beans or beads (yellow, red, white, green) You will need one of each color per child.
- thong for stringing the beads
- 1 stone per child

Goal:
- to help children understand what it means to belong to the family of God
- to confirm and encourage a child's experience of coming into God's family

Objectives:
- for the children to share how they got to know Jesus Christ personally
- to explain God's plan for salvation

Opener *10 minutes*

This activity will help you get aquainted with the children in your class.

1 Spread mural paper on a large table or the wall. You could also use a single sheet of paper for each child.

2 Spread crayons or markers around and invite the children to draw a picture of their family.

3 While they are drawing have them talk about when they were born. As the teacher, you can tell your story too.

4 Before you conclude this activity, give time for each child to explain their drawing.

What makes a family a family?
Take note of their responses; gather ideas from the children and incorporate their insights into the lesson.

Did you know that when we choose to follow Jesus, we become a part of a new family? We even get a new name. Do you know what that name is? It is Christian. It means "little Christ".

1

Teaching/Learning *35 minutes*

Today we are going to tell the stories of how and when we came to be part of God's family. Everyone's story will be different and special.

Teacher Tip

Be sure to affirm something in each child's story.

Activity 1

1 Hand out **Student Guide** and turn to page 6.

2 Invite the children to write about their experience of joining God's family.

or

Invite the children to draw a picture of the place where they became part of God's family.

3 Share stories. Give each child the opportunity to talk about their writing/picture. The leader should share his/her story.

Notes for My Story…

....
....
....
....
....
....
....
....

Now we are going to use colored jelly beans to explain the gift of salvation that brings us into God's family.

Activity 2

1 Spread the jelly beans and stones on the floor or table in front of the children.

2 Have the children take one of each color as well as a stone.

3 Tell the children that the colored beans and the stone can help us describe what happens when we join God's family.

4 Brainstorm, allowing the children to share ideas of what the colored beans could mean and why there is a stone in the middle of the jelly beans.

5 Each color/stone represents part of the salvation experience. Add to the children's ideas with help from the information on pages 12/13.

6 Have children turn to page 8 in the **Student Guide**. Fill in the blanks to describe each part.

Teacher Tip

This may be a good time to change location or position. Invite the children to join you in a circle on a carpet. Leave or collect student books. The books will be used again at the end of Activity 2.

1

Teacher Information:

Red: Reminds us that God <u>loves</u> us

For God so loved the world that he gave his one and only Son, that whoever believes in him shall not perish but have eternal life. John 3:16

God loves us so much that he sent his son, Jesus, to earth from heaven. It was God's plan that Jesus, a perfect person, should die instead of us for the wrong we have done. Red can also remind us of Jesus' blood.

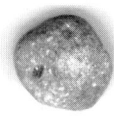

Stone: Reminds us of our <u>sin</u>

All wrongdoing is sin... I John 5:17

A stone does not belong with jelly beans. When we belong to God's family, sin is something that does not belong. God promises that he will forgive our sins. Sin is the wrong things we think and do. It is also the evil in the world. Sin keeps us apart from God.

White: Reminds us that we can have a <u>new</u> <u>start</u>

...wash me and I will be whiter than snow. Psalm 51:7

Jesus did not stay dead. By coming to life again, he showed that he was God and has the power to take away our sin and make us clean.

Teacher Tip

It is not necessary to explain every detail of the salvation plan. Highlight the important facts. The underlined words are the answers to the blanks in the **Student Guide**.

Green: Reminds us that we can <u>grow</u> like trees and grass and <u>learn</u> more about God

But grow in the grace and knowledge of our Lord and Savior Jesus Christ. II Peter 3:18

When we say "yes" to Jesus that means we want to live Jesus' way. It means that we want to know all about him.
I can grow by:
- reading the Bible
- talking to God
- living for God and sharing his love

Yellow: Reminds us of <u>heaven</u>

But our citizenship is in heaven. Philippians 3:20

Heaven is the place where Jesus is now. It is safe, peaceful and beautiful. Because no sin can be there, it is full of light. It is even better than we can imagine. God is getting heaven ready for all who belong to his family.

1

Conclusion 10 minutes

When we choose to join God's family we belong to a new, loving family. The Bible is full of verses that help us know that God loves us. Let's look at some of those verses from the Bible.

Teacher and/or children can read the following verses out loud.

John 3:16
John 14:6
I John 1:9
II Peter 3:18

We are not Christians just because we go to church or because our families read the Bible and pray. These are things Christians do, but they do not make us Christians. We become Christians when we decide to join God's family.

Let the students explore the content of the **Student Guide**. Explain what each of the sections are about.

The Student Guides are for you to use each week. Take them home, but bring them back to the next class. You will use them in class and at home.

"At Home"

Today's "at home" activity can be found on page 9. Write the name of an adult (parent, grandparent, Sunday School teacher, relative) whom you would like to talk to this week.

Ask them these two questions:
- How did you become a Christian?
- What is the best thing about being a Christian?

Encourage the children to fill in the personal information on page 5 of the **Student Guide**.

Notes

2 Getting to Know God

Goal:
- to help children understand that God is awesome and great
- to help children realize that God in all his greatness wants to be their helper

Objectives:
- for the children to discover some facts about God and share them with the class
- for the teacher to guide discussion about who God is

Teacher Preparation

Read: Isaiah 40

God never intended that he would be fully known by us, his creation. Yet he has lovingly provided a variety of ways for us to catch glimpses of who he is – his greatness, his majesty, his justice, his care and his love.

Marvel at the awesome nature of our God.

In this lesson you will be exploring who God is with the children. Bring your wonder and awe with you. Share it with the children so that they can begin to wonder about this amazing God we serve.

Prayer:
If angels bow before you and heaven and earth adore you, how can I do any less? Open my eyes to see the glory of the King of Kings and Lord of Lords. Help me to share your awesomeness with my class. Amen.

What You Need

- **Student Guide** (children should have returned with them)
- white board, black board or newsprint.
- pencils, markers/crayons
- station instruction cards
- extra Bibles

- Dictionary/Bible Dictionary
- tape recorder
- tapes with songs describing God
- a variety of pictures including nature scenes, people, animals, cities etc.

Opener *10 minutes*

Choose one of the following activities to introduce today's lesson.

Teacher Tip
Welcome the children as they come in.

Option #1

Write the word **AWESOME** on the board.
Give me some examples of things or people that are awesome. What makes something or someone awesome?
Write the responses on the board.

God is more awesome than anything or anyone we know. We are going to work at various stations to discover some awesome things about God.

Option #2

Write the word **GOD** on the board.
What do you know about God?
Record key words from their responses.
What would you like to know about God?
Record their questions on the board.

Today we will be exploring and finding out more about who God is.

2

Teaching/Learning *35 minutes*

Children will work at 5 stations and discover ways in which God is awesome.

1 Set up the following five stations before class begins.

2 Write the instructions for each station on a card. Read through the instructions with the children before they go exploring.

3 During class time, the children will move from one station to another to gather information. They can move individually, in two's, three's or as a whole group.

4 Children will need their **Student Guide**, pages 10-12 to record their answers.

Station #1

Read about God in a dictionary.

Supplies for this station:
- dictionary, Bible dictionary
- pens/pencils
- The card for station #1 should include this information:

> **Read about God in a dictionary.**
> Read what the dictionary says to describe God. Write some of these words on page 10 of your **Student Guide**.

Teacher Tip

A children's version of a Bible Dictionary is produced by D.C. Cook, 1993 called *The Picture Bible Dictionary*.

Station #2

The Bible tells us about God.

Supplies for this station:
- Bibles with verses marked with book marks
- pens/pencils
- The card for station #2 should include this information:

Teacher Tip
Use your creativity in designing the station cards.

The Bible tells us about God.
Find out more about God by reading the verses and filling in the blanks on page 10 & 11 in your **Student Guide**.

Answers for Student Guide:
- **Genesis 1:1**
  God <u>made</u> the heavens and the <u>earth</u>.
- **Joshua 1:9**
  God is <u>with</u> you wherever you <u>go</u>.
- **John 5:15-18**
  Jesus can <u>heal</u> sick people.
- **II Corinthians 3:17**
  The Lord our God is the <u>Spirit</u>.
- **Psalm 145:8**
  The Lord is <u>gracious</u> and slow to <u>anger</u>.

2

Station #3

Write a poem of praise to God.

Supplies for this station:
- pens/pencils
- (optional) Psalm of praise - post Psalm 117:1,2 as an example
- The card for station #3 should include this information:

> **Write a poem of praise to God.**
> Write your own words of praise to God by filling in the acrostic on page 11 of your **Student Guide**. Add words that help describe who God is. Match the letters of the word AWESOME with letters in the words of the word list.

Teacher Tip

Here is a list of praise and worship tapes with songs about God.

-*Integrity Music Just for Kids*: King of Kings, Make a Joyful Noise

-*Carmen-Yo Kidz 2*: The Armor of God

Station #4

Songs tell us about God.

Supplies for this station:
- pens/pencils
- tape recorder
- head phones (optional)
- tapes with songs that describe God
- The card for station #4 should include this information:

> **Songs tell us about God.**
> Listen to part of the tape. List some of the words that describe God on page 12 of your **Student Guide**.

Station #5

The world shows us that God is a creator.

Supplies for this station:
- a variety of pictures including nature scenes, people, animals, cities, etc.
- pens/pencils/crayons
- The card for station #5 should include this information:

> **The world shows us that God is a creator.**
> Look at these pictures. God is an awesome creator. On page 12 in your **Student Guide**, draw your own picture of one or more things that God has made.

2

Conclusion *10 minutes*

Invite the children to join you at the table or in a circle on the floor. Ask them to share some of their discoveries about God. If you used Option #2 as your Opener, you may want to refer to the questions that were generated at the beginning of the class. Here are some other questions you could use to guide your discussion:

- Was there anything new that you discovered about God?
- Why is "awesome" a good word to describe God?
- Do you think God knows about you and your life?
- Describe some of your feelings about God.

Teacher Tip

Information given in story form about the character of God can be found in *The Bible Tells Me So* by Mack Thomas, Questar Publishers, 1992 pg. 173-191.

Today we have discovered some special things about God. He is greater and bigger than any of us can imagine. Even his name, I AM, tells us how great he is. His name means that he is forever.

This week when you feel sad, when you feel happy, when you feel strong, or when you feel small and weak – God is with you. He will be with you just as the Bible says.

"At Home"

Highlight for the children the word search on page 13 of the **Student Guide**.

Notes

3 Bible Reading and Prayer

Teacher Preparation
Read: Psalm 119:9-16

The purpose of reading the Bible and praying is to become more intimately acquainted with God. The more we know him, the more we will want to know him.

Psalm 119 is how an author honors the Word of God. It is by learning the Word that we are able to act on it.

Communicating by talking and listening to God is what prayer is all about.

Think about your own reading and prayer life. Are you devoted to getting to know our loving Lord and Savior?

Prayer:
Thank you, Lord God for revealing yourself to me through the Bible. Thank you for the opportunity of communicating with you. Amen.

What You Need
- **Student Guide** (children should have returned with them)
- white board, black board or newsprint
- pencils, markers/crayons
- extra Bibles
- a variety of Bibles: red letter, different versions, picture, other language, tape, computer disk

Goal:
- to motivate children to grow as Christians by talking to God and learning about God

Objectives:
- to understand that the Bible is God's message to us
- to practice using the Bible
- to practice praying

Opener 10 minutes

Choose one of the following activities to introduce today's lesson.

Option #1 Charades
Invite each child to act out an aspect of their favorite Bible story. Have the rest of the class guess which story it is.

Option #2 Drawing
Have each child draw their favorite story and then hold it up for the rest of the class to guess what the story is.

Option #3 Guessing Game
Divide the class into two teams. Ask the following questions, allowing team members to consult each other for the answers. Rotate the questions between teams.

Who Am I? (answer)
- **My mother put me in a reed basket to protect me.** (Moses)
- **I was made out of a rib in order to be Adam's helper.** (Eve)
- **I am the mother of Jesus.** (Mary)
- **When I was young, God spoke to me at night. I thought it was Eli.** (Samuel)
- **I am very short and I climbed a tree to see Jesus.** (Zacchaeus)
- **I was swallowed by a whale.** (Jonah)
- **I wrote many of the Psalms and my best friend was Jonathan.** (David)

3

- I am one of the disciples. My brother Andrew introduced me to Jesus. I also lied about knowing Jesus just before he died. (Peter)
- I prayed three times a day, and landed up in a cage of wild cats! (Daniel)
- My sister's name is Mary. I was angry at her for listening to Jesus instead of helping me with household chores. (Martha)

Where do these stories come from? Did any of these characters talk to God? Did God talk to any of them? The Bible is full of many exciting stories. Today we are going to learn about reading the Bible and prayer.

Teaching/Learning *35 minutes*

Activity 1 Bible Reading

1 Invite the children to sit around the table with you.

2 When we grow as Christians, we want to get to know Jesus better. He is like a new friend. We need to spend time together with him. He is a good friend who will never go away.

Have the children share ideas about how to make a friend. Listen for ideas like: talking together, playing together, phoning each other, writing notes or letters to each other, doing special things together.

3 Explain what the Bible is.
The Bible is like a long letter that God has written to us. It tells us about the things he has done and about people he knows. It also tells us about how we should act when we belong to God's family.

Teacher Tip
Provide extra Bibles in case a child does not have one. See the Resource List for recommended Children's Bibles.

4 Examine some Bibles.
Turn to page 14 in the **Student Guide**. Provide a variety of Bibles. Let the children take a look at the Bibles.
Are all the Bibles exactly the same?
What makes them different? How are they the same?
Here are some Bible Facts: (Underlined items are answers to blanks on page 14 of the **Student Guide**)
- <u>66</u> books in the Bible
- 39 in the Old Testament
- 27 in the New Testament
- it took about <u>1,600</u> years to write it
- the Bible is like God's <u>letter</u> to us

5 Practice finding a verse or a story in the Bible.
Turn to pages 14 & 15 in the **Student Guide**.
When we read the Bible by ourselves or together, we have to know how to find what we want to read. References help us do that.
Use the example (John 3:16) in the **Student Guide**, pages 14 & 15.

Teacher Tip
Some children will be very familiar with the Bible and will be able to find chapter and verse. Others will not know how to do this at all.

- Show them how to find 'John' in the Table of Contents. Help them locate the page number.
- Turn to that page in their Bibles.
- Show the children that the book is divided into chapters. Invite the children to find chapter 3.
- Show the children that each chapter is divided into verses. Invite the children to find verse 16.
- Ask several of the children to read what they have found.
- Practice the exercise again by providing some of your own references. Remind the children to start with the Table of Contents, turn to the Book, find the chapter and then the verse.

3

6 Reading the Bible *(optional)*
The Bible is full of many exciting stories. These stories help us know about God and Jesus. The Bible helps us to know how to live.
- **Let's read a story together.** (Choose a story from the list of stories on page 36 in the Student Guide). **Turn to the reference in your Bible.**
- Read the story out loud together.
- Encourage them to help each other: **To help us understand what the Bible tells us to do, we can ask some questions.**
  - **Does this story tell me something to do?**
  - **Does this story tell me to stop doing something?**
  - **What does this story tell me about God?**
- Discuss the responses. Remind the children that there will not always be answers for each question in each story.

Activity 2 Prayer

1 If possible, move to a new location in the room.

2 To get to know God, we can read the Bible and we can pray.

**Have you ever heard anyone pray?
What do people say in their prayers?
What could you say to God?**

Listen to the children's responses. Remind the children that:
- God likes it when we talk to him.
- We can pray anywhere, anytime.

- God always hears us.
- God likes to hear about the happy things in our lives as well as the hard, sad or problem times.

3 Turn in the **Student Guide** to page 16
Write the word **PRAY** on the board as it is written in the **Student Guide**. Fill in the blanks during the following discussion.

Now we are going to learn about talking to God. On page 16 of your Student Guide you have the word PRAY. Each letter reminds us of something we could talk to God about. Let's fill in the blanks.

As you help the children with the answers, include some examples of what each means. Write these examples on the board. You will use these when you pray with the children in Step #4.

P - praise   means thanking God for the good things he does.

R - repent   means telling God I am sorry for the wrongs I have done.

A - ask   means asking God to help.

Y - yes   is saying "yes" to God for what he wants me to do.

3

Teacher Tip
Remind the children that God listens to our prayers regardless of our posture. The reason we often close our eyes and fold our hands is to show respect and focus our attention.

4 Pray, using the acrostic guideline from the board.
God hears us no matter where we are. We can show that we think he is great by folding our hands, bowing our heads and closing our eyes. But God hears us even if we keep our eyes open. Today we are going to pray together.

If you need help remembering words, you can look at the board.

I will start each part of our prayer, and you can add to what I say. Use some of the words on the board to help you. I invite you to pray out loud.

Teacher:
Dear God, I praise you for:
(allow children to fill in with their own words)
Dear God, I repent of:
Dear God, I ask you to help me:
Dear God, I want to say yes about:
In Jesus' name I pray, Amen.

Conclusion 5 minutes

Reading your Bible and talking to God will be things that you will do as long as you continue to love Jesus and want to follow him. It will be two of the ways you find out more about him and how to please him.

"At Home"

Turn to page 36 in the **Student Guide**, to find a list of Bible stories. Encourage the children to read two or three this week. Show them that they can record what they read about on page 17.

Show them pages 18 & 19 and encourage them to use these pages to pray.

Notes

4 Belonging at Church

Goal:
- for children to understand that they are part of the Church, the Body of Christ

Objectives:
- for the children to tour the church building to see the functions of the Church
- for the children to discover how they can contribute to and receive from the Body

Teacher Preparation
Read I Corinthians 12:12-30

Every once in awhile we need an object lesson to understand a concept. That is what Paul has given us in his letter to the Corinthian church. The Church is described as a body. All of us know that a body with all of its parts functioning correctly does what a body needs to do.

In the Church there are different parts or gifts that need to function together so that the cause of Jesus Christ can be proclaimed. You are part of that Church.

Prayer:
Jesus Christ, I honor you as the head of the Church. Your plan is that each of us may function within the Body so that the world may see you.

Thank you that the children of this class are also part of the Body. May they begin to see how they can give and receive as they grow in this Body. Amen.

What You Need

- **Student Guide** (children should have returned with them)
- puzzle (50 pieces or less)
  or
  recipe ingredients
- white board, blackboard or newsprint

- pencils, markers/crayons
- extra Bibles
- letter to parents (see note on page 39)

Opener *10 minutes*

This is the last session of these lessons. As you welcome the children to class let them know that you are glad they have been with you. Choose one of the following activities to introduce today's lesson.

Option #1 Puzzle

Randomly give out the pieces of the puzzle to each of the students. Put the puzzle together.

Option #2 Recipe

Use a 'nuts and bolts' recipe or non-baking trail mix recipe. Gather the ingredients and have everyone participate in putting the recipe together. If it takes some cooking or baking, that can be done during the lesson. Then you'll have a snack for the end of the session.

The activity we have just done shows us that when we work together we can do amazing things. If we had left out one puzzle piece (or one ingredient) something would have been missing. Each of you was important and needed.

In our time together today, we are going to see that it is just the same in the Church. The Church works together to get the job done.

4

Teaching/Learning *30 minutes*

When you became a Christian, you joined a new family. You are still part of the family you live with here, but you are also part of a much larger family. It's called the Church.

Teacher Tip
Take the time to explain that often Church (with capital C) means the people, and church (small c) means the church building. This may be a bit difficult for the youngest children, but worth the effort.

1 Write the word **CHURCH** on the board. Ask the children to share with you whatever comes to their minds when they hear or see the word church. Record their answers on the board.

The Church is much more than a building. It includes all those who belong to the family of God. This means that people who are believers in God anywhere in the world belong to the Church like we do.

2 Invite the children to turn in their Bibles to:
  - I Corinthians 12:14-22
  - I Corinthians 12:24b-27

The Bible uses picture language to help us understand what the church is like. Take turns reading the verses.

The Bible tells us in these verses that the Church is like a body. A body is made up of arms, legs, eyes, ears. Each part of the body has a different job to do. In the Church there are different kinds of things that need to be done too. Some people lead singing, teach Sunday School or clubs, some sing, some talk, some usher. Everyone is needed in the Church.

3 During this activity take the children on a tour of several places in the church building. At each place explain what the children can give and receive at that location. If you can, invite the pastor(s), church secretary, choir/worship leader, usher, etc. to meet you at their place of involvement to answer questions.

Children will need to bring their **Student Guides** (pages 20 - 23) and pencils.

The order of the walk is up to you. Begin where it is most suitable for you. Here are some suggested locations with questions to ask the children.

Teacher Tip

The answers in the 'church walk' are personal experience. But it can also encourage children to begin thinking differently about coming to the church building and being with the Church.

Entrance
Go to the entrance through which most of the children would enter the church.
When we come to meet with other Christians we should come thinking about what we can give or receive.

What could you receive at Church?
- a bulletin, Sunday School paper
- an answer to a problem or question
- information about being a Christian

Affirm the answers and help the children discover that we come to worship and get to know God better.

What could you give at Church?
- your offering
- your life to God
- a listening attitude
- a smile and being a friend
- thanks to God for what he has done.

Affirm their answers and help them discover that we come to praise God and give help to others.

4

Teacher Tip

There may be symbols in your worship place that you want to explain - a banner, a cross, the pulpit, the communion table.

Worship Area

(Go to the sanctuary or worship area)
This is the place where people who love God come together to worship and learn more about him. God wants us to give thanks for the good things he has done. He wants us to enjoy our relationship with him.

What can you give in this room?
- attention to what is happening
- thanks to God by singing and praying
- your offering

What can you receive in this room?
- the opportunity to get to know God better
- answers to questions
- encouragement

Stage

(Go to the front of the worship area)
When people get together to worship, there are those who help us know what we should do. They usually stand at the front of the room. These people lead worship and singing. They talk about what is happening in our church and they give a talk or preach a sermon.

What do the people give at the front of this room?
- their gifts and talents (playing musical instruments, singing, speaking, drama)
- their ideas about following Jesus
- instructions and information about what is happening at the church

Church Office
(Go to the area of the church office(s))
Did you know that many more activities happen at the church than what happens on Sunday morning or evening?

What are some of the other kinds of meetings that happen during the week?
- club programs
- choir practice
- youth meetings
- Bible studies
- moms or ladies meetings
- church business meetings

Explain that each of these meetings help people to work together in the Church and to understand what it means to be part of God's family.

If a pastor is unavailable, help the children understand the many kinds of jobs that pastors do. (They study the Bible so they can preach a sermon, pray for the Church, visit people who need help or are sick and they help people by doing weddings and funerals.)

Sunday School Room
(Go back to your classroom)
Our church has many Sunday School rooms where adults and children meet together in small groups to learn about Jesus. Each class has a leader who helps others learn.

4

What can you give in your Sunday School class?
- attention
- ideas and answers
- friendship
- offering

What can you receive in your Sunday School class?
- stories about Jesus
- ideas about growing and loving God more

More...
You may also want to visit other areas in your church building that could help the children understand the importance of being part of this congregation. Other areas might be the kitchen, library, gym etc.

Today we have learned something about our church building and the people who are part of it. When we are part of God's family, we all belong to the Church. Each one of us has something to give. As you grow up you will learn new ways to give and to receive. You are an important member of the Church body.

Conclusion *10 minutes*

We have come to the end of our classes together. During these lessons, I hope you have learned some new things about what it means to be a Christian at your age. I hope you leave this class knowing that Jesus is your best friend and that he always wants to be with you.

"At Home"

Point out the "My Journal" section in the **Student Guide** (pages 24-35). Encourage the children to use these activities to continue their walk with Jesus.

If there is time, you may want to ask their reflections on the class. Affirm their faith and remind them that they can be an encouragement to each other.

Final Note to Teachers

It is a good idea to send a letter of information and encouragement to the parents of the class members.

Include information about the topics covered in the class and a description of other programs the child could participate in at the church. Inform them that you can be contacted if they have further questions.

Teacher Tip

If you had some children new to your church as part of your class, be sure to invite them to attend Sunday School. Introduce them to their class and to their teacher.

Notes

Resource List

General Resources

Chapin, Alice *Building Your Child's Faith* Nashville: Thomas Nelson Publishers, 1990.

Davis, Jr., Cos H. *Children and the Christian Faith* Nashville: Broadman Press, 1990.

Owen, Herb *How to Shepherd Children in a World Full of Wolves* Lynchburg: Church Growth Institute, 1993.

Thomas, Mack *The Bible Tells Me So* Sisters: Questar Publishers, 1992.

Devotional Resources

Barclift, Stephen T. *The Beginner's Devotional* Sisters: Questar Publishing, Inc., 1991.

Cook, Janice and Kathy Comina *The Family Bible Companion* Downer's Grove: InterVarsity Press, 1991.

Harmon, Jeannie, editor *Awesome Real Life Bible Devotions for Kids* Elgin: Chariot Books, D.C. Cook Publishing Co., 1991.

Bible Resources

The Adventure Bible, New International Version - published by Zondervan.

The Wonder Bible, selections from the International Children's Bible - published by Questar.

The Youth Bible, New Century Version - published by Word/Group.

Sample Letter

Date

Dear Parent/Guardian

I am excited about the spiritual growth opportunities at (**name of your church**). Children are finding these opportunities in Sunday School, Pioneer Clubs, VBS (**name the programs offered by your church**). They are getting to know about God through these ministries and many of them are making decisions to follow Jesus.

Teacher Tip

Send this letter to all parents who have children between the ages of 7-11.

During (**dates of the First Steps program**), I would like to invite children who have made a commitment to Jesus Christ to a class called First Steps for Kids. I would like to meet with a maximum of 10 kids during the (**time of class**) for four weeks. These classes are voluntary and will be advertised during Sunday School. I will invite the children to fill in a form and hand it to me if they are interested in attending.

The purpose of these classes is to enable children to talk about the decision they have made for God. It is also to guide them in taking further steps in their walk with Jesus. I want to encourage them to get to know God. We will talk about how to read the Bible and pray and we'll also explore what it means to be part of the church.

If you have any questions about this program, please feel f ree to call. I am looking forward to growing with your children!

(name of the First Steps teacher)

Sample Letter to Invite the Children to Participate

COME JOIN A CLASS CALLED

Teacher Tip

Give this letter to every child between the ages of 7-11 and explain to them what the program is all about. In the letter that you prepare use the First Steps logo (a larger version to copy and paste is located on the Title page). Allow for a portion to be cut off and returned with information.

Have you made a decision to follow Jesus?
Do you want to know more about being a Christian?
Do you ever wonder what the church is all about?

If you are interested in talking and learning about being the best Christian you can be then fill in the form below.

We will have a special class for four weeks (**dates**) in room (**location**).

-- ✂

First Steps for Kids

I would like to come to the class.

My name is: ....

My phone number is: ....

Please give this form to
(**the name of the First Steps teacher**)

About the Author

Lorraine Dick has been involved in Christian education ministries for many years in Mennonite Brethren churches in Canada, camps, and as a short term missionary in South America.

Lorraine developed **First Steps for Kids** in response to a need in her CE ministry at the Waterloo Mennonite Brethren church. Many children were making decisions at camp and Vacation Bible School, and needed follow up. In addition, many adults were being won to Christ through the ministry of the church, and their children needed some orientation to new behaviors at home (not to mention having to go to church on Sunday!).

With her winsome personality, Lorraine drew children to herself and to Jesus. This publication of **First Steps for Kids** is an attempt to pass on the immense success of her personal ministry to others in Christian education.